THE PSYCHOLOGY OF INVESTING

Overcoming Biases and Making Smarter Decisions

By

Dr. Paul .C. Ajulufoh

© 2024 Dr. Paul C. Ajulufoh
All rights reserved.

No part of this book may be reproduced, distributed, or transmitted in any form or by any means without the prior written permission of the author, except in the case of brief quotations embodied in critical reviews and certain other noncommercial uses permitted by copyright law.

ISBN: 979-8335419765

Disclaimer: The information provided in this book is for educational purposes only and does not constitute financial advice. The author is not liable for any losses or damages associated with the use of this book.

Self-published via Amazon Kindle Direct Publishing

Table of Content

Introduction
- Importance of understanding psychology in investing
- Overview of common biases and their impact on investment decisions

Chapter 1: The Foundations of Behavioral Finance
- Definition and history of behavioral finance
- Key concepts and theories
- Difference between traditional and behavioral finance

Chapter 2: Common Cognitive Biases in Investing
- Overconfidence bias
- Confirmation bias
- Anchoring
- Loss aversion
- Herd behavior

Chapter 3: Emotional Influences on Investment Decisions
- Fear and greed
- Impact of stress and anxiety
- The role of personality in investment choices

Chapter 4: The Psychology of Risk and Uncertainty
- Perception of risk
- Risk tolerance and risk capacity
- Strategies for managing risk

Chapter 5: Decision-Making Strategies
- Rational vs. irrational decision-making
- Techniques to improve decision-making
- The role of intuition in investing

Chapter 6: Overcoming Biases

- Identifying personal biases
- Strategies to mitigate biases
- Case studies of successful investors

Chapter 7: Practical Applications and Tools
- Using technology to reduce biases
- Tools for better decision-making
- Building a bias-resistant investment strategy

Conclusion
- Recap of key points
- Encouragement for continuous learning and improvement

INTRODUCTION

Importance of Understanding Psychology in Investing

Investing is often perceived as a game of numbers, charts, and financial statements. However, beneath the surface of these tangible metrics lies a powerful force that significantly influences investment decisions: psychology. Understanding the psychological aspects of investing is crucial for anyone looking to achieve long-term success in the financial markets.

The Hidden Influencers Psychological factors often operate subconsciously, guiding decisions in ways that may not align with logical analysis. These factors can lead to irrational behavior, resulting in missed opportunities or costly mistakes. By understanding the underlying psychological drivers, investors can develop strategies to mitigate their influence and make more rational decisions.

Behavioral Finance: Bridging the Gap Behavioral finance, a field that combines psychology and economics, explores how cognitive biases and emotional responses affect financial decisions. It challenges the traditional assumption that investors are always rational and markets are always efficient. By acknowledging and studying these irrational behaviors, behavioral finance provides insights into why markets move the way they do and how investors can better navigate them.

Enhancing Decision-Making Skills A solid grasp of investment psychology equips investors with tools to recognize and counteract their biases. It fosters a disciplined approach to investing, helping individuals stick to their strategies even during volatile market conditions. Understanding one's psychological tendencies can lead to more thoughtful decision-making, ultimately enhancing investment performance.

The Role of Emotions in Investing Emotions such as fear and greed play a significant role in investment decisions. Fear can lead to panic selling during market downturns, while greed can drive irrational exuberance during bull markets. By recognizing these emotional triggers, investors can take steps to manage their responses and avoid making impulsive decisions based on short-term market movements.

Long-Term Perspective Investing is a marathon, not a sprint. Psychological resilience and a long-term perspective are vital for weathering market fluctuations and achieving financial goals. Understanding the psychological challenges that arise throughout the investment journey can help investors stay focused and committed to their long-term plans.

Overview of Common Biases and Their Impact on Investment Decisions

Cognitive biases are systematic patterns of deviation from norm or rationality in judgment, which often lead to illogical and suboptimal decisions. In the context of investing, these biases can significantly impact an investor's ability to make sound financial decisions. Here, we explore some of the most common biases and their effects on investing.

Overconfidence Bias Overconfidence bias is the tendency to overestimate one's knowledge, abilities, and the precision of one's information. In investing, this can lead to excessive trading, underestimating risks, and ultimately, poorer performance. Overconfident investors may believe they can consistently outperform the market, leading to a false sense of security and significant losses.

Confirmation Bias Confirmation bias refers to the tendency to search for, interpret, and remember information in a way that confirms one's preconceptions. Investors affected by this bias might ignore or undervalue evidence that contradicts their existing beliefs, leading to poor decision-making. For instance, an investor may hold onto a losing stock because they selectively focus on positive news while disregarding negative indicators.

Anchoring Anchoring is the reliance on the first piece of information encountered (the "anchor") when making decisions. In investing, this can manifest as an undue emphasis on the initial price paid for a stock. Investors might hold onto losing investments, hoping they will "bounce back" to their original purchase price, rather than evaluating the stock based on its current fundamentals.

Loss Aversion Loss aversion is the tendency to prefer avoiding losses rather than acquiring equivalent gains. It suggests that the pain of losing is psychologically twice as powerful as the pleasure of gaining. This bias can lead investors to make overly conservative decisions, such as selling winning investments too early to "lock in" gains or avoiding investments with higher potential returns due to fear of loss.

Herd Behavior Herd behavior describes the tendency to follow and mimic the actions of a larger group, whether rational or irrational. In investing, this can lead to bubble formations or panic selling. Investors might buy into a rising market because others are doing so (fear of missing out), or sell during a downturn because everyone else is, regardless of their long-term investment strategy.

The Impact on Investment Outcomes Understanding these biases is the first step toward mitigating their impact. Investors who are aware of their cognitive biases can take proactive steps to counteract them, such as setting predetermined rules for buying and selling, diversifying their portfolios, and seeking out contrarian viewpoints to challenge their assumptions.

Strategies for Overcoming Biases

- **Education and Awareness**: Continual learning about common biases and their effects can help investors recognize when they are falling prey to these tendencies.

- **Objective Decision-Making**: Using checklists and predefined criteria for investment decisions can reduce the influence of emotions and biases.
- **Diversification**: A well-diversified portfolio can help mitigate the risks associated with individual biases, as it spreads risk across different assets and sectors.
- **Seeking Professional Advice**: Financial advisors and investment professionals can provide an objective perspective and help investors stay disciplined.

By understanding and addressing these psychological factors, investors can improve their decision-making processes, enhance their investment performance, and achieve more consistent, long-term success in the financial markets.

CHAPTER 1

The Foundations of Behavioral Finance

Behavioral finance is a subfield of finance that explores how psychological influences and cognitive biases affect the financial behaviors of investors and financial practitioners. Unlike traditional finance, which assumes that individuals are rational actors who make decisions solely based on logical analysis and available information, behavioral finance acknowledges that humans often behave irrationally due to psychological factors.

At its core, behavioral finance seeks to understand the "why" behind investors' decisions. It combines insights from various disciplines, including psychology, sociology, and conventional finance, to explain behaviors that deviate from the expected rational models. For example, it looks at why investors might hold onto losing stocks for too long, why they follow market trends without sufficient analysis, or why they might overreact to news.

Key Components of Behavioral Finance

1. **Psychological Influences**: These include emotions such as fear, greed, and hope, which can drive investors to make irrational decisions. Emotional reactions

to market movements, news, and personal financial situations often lead to suboptimal investment choices.
2. **Cognitive Biases**: These are systematic patterns of deviation from norm or rationality in judgment. Common biases include overconfidence, anchoring, and loss aversion, which lead investors to make decisions that are not aligned with traditional financial theories.
3. **Heuristics**: Mental shortcuts or rules of thumb that people use to make quick decisions. While heuristics can be helpful in everyday life, they can lead to significant errors in judgment in complex fields like finance.
4. **Market Anomalies**: Behavioral finance explains phenomena that traditional finance cannot, such as market bubbles, crashes, and anomalies in asset pricing. These events often result from collective irrational behavior and herd mentality.

Application of Behavioral Finance

Behavioral finance is not just theoretical; it has practical applications in areas like portfolio management, financial planning, and policy-making. By understanding the psychological factors at play, financial professionals can better predict market movements, create more effective investment strategies, and help investors avoid common pitfalls.

History

The development of behavioral finance can be traced back through several key phases and contributions from various scholars and researchers. Its evolution has challenged the traditional notions of finance and provided a richer understanding of market dynamics and investor behavior.

Early 20th Century Foundations

The early 20th century laid the groundwork for behavioral finance through pioneering work in psychology and economics:

- **Sigmund Freud**: Freud's theories on the unconscious

mind and human behavior influenced the understanding of irrational actions. While not directly related to finance, his ideas on human psychology set the stage for later explorations into irrational financial behavior.

- **B.F. Skinner**: As a behaviorist, Skinner's work on operant conditioning and behavior modification highlighted how external stimuli and reinforcements could influence behavior. This contributed to the understanding of how market news and events might condition investor responses.

Mid-20th Century Developments

The mid-20th century saw the introduction of key concepts that would later become integral to behavioral finance:

- **Herbert Simon (1950s-60s)**: Simon introduced the concept of "bounded rationality," which suggests that individuals are rational within the limits of their information and cognitive capacity. This concept challenged the idea of perfect rationality in economic models and highlighted the limitations faced by real-world decision-makers.

Key Contributions of the 1970s

The 1970s were transformative for behavioral finance, thanks to groundbreaking work by psychologists and economists:

- **Daniel Kahneman and Amos Tversky**: Their research on cognitive biases and heuristics revolutionized the understanding of decision-making processes. They developed the **prospect theory**, which describes how people evaluate potential losses and gains and how they make decisions under risk. This theory demonstrated that people are not always rational actors and that their decisions are influenced by cognitive biases and psychological factors.

Key Concepts from Prospect Theory:

- **Loss Aversion**: People tend to prefer avoiding losses to acquiring equivalent gains. This means the pain of losing is felt more strongly than the pleasure of gaining.
- **Reference Points**: Individuals evaluate outcomes relative to a reference point (often the status quo) rather than in absolute terms.
- **Diminishing Sensitivity**: As the size of gains or losses increases, the marginal impact on utility diminishes.

1980s and Beyond: The Rise of Behavioral Finance

The 1980s and subsequent decades saw the formal establishment and growth of behavioral finance as a recognized field within economics and finance:

- **Richard Thaler**: Often regarded as the father of behavioral finance, Thaler's work on anomalies and biases in decision-making further integrated psychology with economics. His research on the "endowment effect," "mental accounting," and other concepts illustrated how people's irrational behavior could be systematically studied and predicted.
- **Integration into Mainstream Economics**: The growing body of evidence from behavioral studies began to influence mainstream economics. Traditional models of rational behavior were increasingly supplemented or replaced by models that accounted for psychological influences.

Nobel Prizes and Academic Recognition

The recognition of behavioral finance as a critical field in economics was solidified by several key accolades:

- **Daniel Kahneman (2002 Nobel Prize)**: Kahneman was awarded the Nobel Prize in Economic Sciences for his work on integrating psychological research into economic science, especially concerning human judgment and decision-making under uncertainty. This recognition marked a significant milestone in the acceptance of behavioral finance within the broader economics community.

- **Richard Thaler (2017 Nobel Prize)**: Thaler received the Nobel Prize for his contributions to behavioral economics, particularly his insights into how human behavior deviates from traditional economic assumptions.

Continued Evolution and Impact

Today, behavioral finance continues to evolve, incorporating new findings from psychology, neuroscience, and behavioral economics. Its principles are applied in various domains, including investment management, corporate finance, public policy, and personal financial planning. Financial professionals increasingly use behavioral insights to design better products, improve client outcomes, and enhance decision-making processes.

By acknowledging and studying the psychological factors that influence financial decisions, behavioral finance provides a more comprehensive understanding of market dynamics and investor behavior. It bridges the gap between theory and practice, offering valuable insights that help investors make more informed and rational decisions in an inherently complex and unpredictable financial world.

CHAPTER 2

Common Cognitive Biases in Investing

Cognitive biases are systematic patterns of deviation from rationality that affect our judgments and decisions. In investing, these biases can lead to suboptimal financial outcomes. This chapter explores some of the most common cognitive biases and their impact on investment decisions.

Overconfidence Bias

Definition Overconfidence bias is the tendency for people to overestimate their knowledge, abilities, and the accuracy of their information. This bias leads investors to believe they are better at predicting market movements and picking stocks than they actually are.

Impact on Investing

- **Excessive Trading**: Overconfident investors trade more frequently, believing they can consistently outperform the market. This results in higher transaction costs and can erode returns.
- **Underestimating Risks**: Overconfident investors often take on more risk than they should, underestimating the probability of adverse outcomes.
- **Ignoring Advice**: Overconfident investors may

disregard professional advice or contrary evidence, believing their own analysis is superior.

Examples

- **Individual Investors**: An individual investor might consistently trade based on their market predictions, often leading to poorer performance compared to a passive investment strategy.
- **Fund Managers**: A fund manager might overestimate their ability to pick winning stocks, leading to a portfolio that is riskier and less diversified.

Case Study: The Fall of Long-Term Capital Management In the 1990s, Long-Term Capital Management (LTCM) was a hedge fund led by highly confident traders and Nobel Prize-winning economists. They believed their sophisticated models could consistently outperform the market. However, their overconfidence led to excessive leverage and underestimation of risk. In 1998, the fund nearly collapsed, requiring a bailout to prevent a broader financial crisis.

Confirmation Bias

Definition Confirmation bias is the tendency to search for, interpret, and remember information in a way that confirms one's preexisting beliefs or hypotheses. This leads to the selective gathering of evidence that supports one's views while ignoring contradictory information.

Impact on Investing

- **Reinforcing Misconceptions**: Investors might hold onto erroneous beliefs about a stock or market trend, leading to poor investment decisions.
- **Resistance to New Information**: Confirmation bias makes it difficult for investors to adapt to new information that contradicts their existing views.
- **Increased Volatility**: When many investors exhibit confirmation bias, it can lead to overreactions to news

and increased market volatility.

Examples

- **Holding onto Losing Stocks**: An investor might continue to hold onto a losing stock, focusing only on positive news and ignoring negative indicators.
- **Selective News Consumption**: An investor might only follow news sources that align with their market outlook, reinforcing their biases.

Case Study: The Dot-Com Bubble During the late 1990s, many investors were convinced that internet companies would continue to grow exponentially. They focused on positive news and growth projections while ignoring signs of overvaluation and weak business models. This confirmation bias contributed to the formation and eventual burst of the dot-com bubble, leading to massive losses.

Anchoring Bias

Definition Anchoring bias is the reliance on the first piece of information encountered (the "anchor") when making decisions. In investing, this often manifests as an undue emphasis on the initial purchase price of an investment.

Impact on Investing

- **Holding onto Investments**: Investors may hold onto a losing investment, anchored to the initial purchase price and waiting for it to recover, even when it would be more rational to sell.
- **Mispricing Assets**: Anchoring can lead to mispricing assets, as investors may rely too heavily on past prices or initial estimates rather than current market conditions.

Examples

- **Stock Prices**: An investor might refuse to sell a stock that has dropped in value, waiting for it to return to its original purchase price despite negative market trends.
- **Earnings Estimates**: Analysts may stick to their initial

earnings estimates for a company, even in the face of new information that suggests a significant change.

Case Study: Housing Market Crisis Many homeowners during the 2008 financial crisis were anchored to the initial purchase prices of their homes. Despite market conditions indicating a decline in home values, they held onto their properties, hoping prices would rebound to their original levels. This anchoring bias led to delayed sales and increased financial distress as home values continued to fall.

Loss Aversion

Definition Loss aversion is the tendency for people to prefer avoiding losses rather than acquiring equivalent gains. It suggests that the pain of losing is psychologically twice as powerful as the pleasure of gaining.

Impact on Investing

- **Conservative Investment Choices**: Investors might choose overly conservative investments to avoid potential losses, missing out on higher returns.
- **Premature Selling**: Investors might sell winning investments too early to "lock in" gains, driven by the fear of losing those gains.
- **Holding onto Losers**: Conversely, investors might hold onto losing investments for too long, hoping to avoid realizing a loss.

Examples

- **Stock Market**: During a market downturn, an investor might sell stocks prematurely to avoid further losses, potentially missing out on a market rebound.
- **Real Estate**: A homeowner might refuse to sell a property at a loss, holding onto it even if the market conditions are unfavorable.

Case Study: Investor Behavior During Market Corrections During market corrections, many investors sell their stocks to avoid further losses, driven by loss aversion. This behavior often leads to selling at the bottom of the market and missing out on subsequent recoveries, resulting in lower overall returns compared to those who stayed invested.

Herd Behavior

Definition Herd behavior describes the tendency to follow and mimic the actions of a larger group, whether rational or irrational. In investing, this can lead to bubble formations or panic selling.

Impact on Investing

- **Market Bubbles**: Herd behavior can drive asset prices to unsustainable levels, creating bubbles that eventually burst.
- **Panic Selling**: During market downturns, herd behavior can lead to widespread panic selling, exacerbating market declines.
- **Reduced Individual Analysis**: Investors following the herd may neglect their own analysis and due diligence, leading to poor investment choices.

Examples

- **Dot-Com Bubble**: In the late 1990s, herd behavior drove up the prices of internet stocks to unsustainable levels, leading to the eventual burst of the dot-com bubble.
- **Financial Crisis of 2008**: Herd behavior contributed to the housing bubble and subsequent financial crisis, as investors and institutions followed each other into high-risk mortgage-backed securities.

Case Study: Bitcoin Mania The rapid rise of Bitcoin and other cryptocurrencies in 2017 showcased herd behavior. Many investors, driven by FOMO (fear of missing out), bought into cryptocurrencies without understanding the underlying technology or risks. This herd behavior led to a massive bubble that eventually burst, causing significant losses for latecomers.

The Impact on Investment Outcomes

Understanding these biases is the first step toward mitigating their impact. Investors who are aware of their cognitive biases can take proactive steps to counteract them, such as setting predetermined rules for buying and selling, diversifying their portfolios, and seeking out contrarian viewpoints to challenge their assumptions.

Case Study: Value Investing Strategy Value investors, such as those following Warren Buffett's principles, focus on the intrinsic value of investments rather than market trends or herd behavior. By adhering to a disciplined approach and conducting thorough analysis, they can avoid common biases and achieve long-term success.

Strategies for Overcoming Biases

Education and Awareness Continual learning about common biases and their effects can help investors recognize when they are falling prey to these tendencies. This includes staying informed about psychological research and market trends.

Objective Decision-Making Using checklists and predefined criteria for investment decisions can reduce the influence of emotions and biases. For example, establishing rules for when to sell a stock can prevent irrational decisions based on short-term market movements.

Diversification A well-diversified portfolio can help mitigate the risks associated with individual biases, as it spreads risk across different assets and sectors. Diversification reduces the impact of any single investment decision on the overall portfolio.

Seeking Professional Advice Financial advisors and investment professionals can provide an objective perspective and help investors stay disciplined. Advisors can offer insights that are not influenced by the investor's personal biases.

Regular Review and Adjustment Periodically reviewing and adjusting one's investment strategy can help ensure it remains aligned with long-term goals and not driven by short-term biases. This includes reassessing risk tolerance and investment objectives.

Case Study: Regular Portfolio Rebalancing An investor who regularly reviews and rebalances their portfolio can ensure that it remains aligned with their risk tolerance and investment goals. For instance, if a particular asset class becomes overrepresented due to market gains, rebalancing can help maintain the desired asset allocation and reduce exposure to potential biases.

By understanding and addressing these cognitive biases, investors can improve their decision-making processes, enhance their investment performance, and achieve more consistent, long-term success in the financial markets.

CHAPTER 3

Emotional Influences on Investment Decisions

Investing is not just a numbers game; it's heavily influenced by human emotions. Fear, greed, stress, anxiety, and personality traits all play crucial roles in shaping investment decisions. Understanding these emotional influences can help investors make more rational decisions and achieve better financial outcomes.

Fear and Greed

Definition Fear and greed are two of the most influential emotions that drive investment decisions. Fear often results in panic selling and overly cautious investment behavior, while greed can lead to speculative bubbles and high-risk investments. These emotions can cloud judgment, leading to decisions that are not based on rational analysis.

Impact on Investing

- **Fear**: Fear can cause investors to sell assets prematurely during market downturns, resulting in realized losses and missed opportunities for recovery. It can lead to an overly conservative investment approach, which may prevent investors from taking advantage of potential gains.

- **Greed**: Greed can drive investors to take excessive risks, invest in speculative assets, and participate in market bubbles. This behavior can lead to significant losses when the bubble bursts or when the speculative investments do not perform as expected.

Examples

- **Market Crashes**: During the 2008 financial crisis, widespread fear led to a massive sell-off in the stock market, causing prices to plummet. Investors, driven by fear, sold their assets at a loss, contributing to the market decline.
- **Dot-Com Boom**: In the late 1990s, rampant speculation driven by greed led investors to pour money into tech stocks without regard to fundamentals. This irrational exuberance caused stock prices to soar, creating a bubble that eventually burst, leading to substantial financial losses for many investors.

Case Study: The Bitcoin Bubble The rapid rise in Bitcoin's price in 2017 is another example of greed-driven investment. As Bitcoin's price soared, more and more investors jumped on the bandwagon, hoping to make quick profits. The fear of missing out (FOMO) further fueled the buying frenzy. When the bubble burst, Bitcoin's price plummeted, and many investors who bought at the peak suffered significant losses.

Impact of Stress and Anxiety

Definition Stress and anxiety are emotional responses to perceived threats or uncertainties. In the context of investing, these emotions can arise from market volatility, financial losses, or economic instability. Stress and anxiety can impair decision-making processes, leading to suboptimal investment choices.

Impact on Investing

- **Poor Decision-Making**: High levels of stress and anxiety can impair cognitive function, leading to irrational decisions and reactionary behavior. Investors

under stress may make hasty decisions without fully considering the implications.
- **Avoidance Behavior**: Investors experiencing high levels of stress might avoid making necessary decisions altogether, resulting in missed opportunities or failure to mitigate risks. This avoidance can lead to a lack of portfolio adjustments during critical times.

Examples
- **Avoiding Investment Opportunities**: An investor might avoid investing in the stock market during volatile periods due to anxiety, missing out on potential gains when the market recovers. This can result in lower overall returns and missed opportunities for growth.
- **Panic Selling**: An investor might sell off assets at the first sign of market decline due to stress-induced panic, locking in losses instead of waiting for a recovery. This knee-jerk reaction can lead to significant financial losses.

Case Study: The COVID-19 Pandemic The COVID-19 pandemic caused unprecedented levels of market volatility, leading to widespread stress and anxiety among investors. Many panicked and sold their investments at the height of the market crash in March 2020. Those who held onto their investments, however, saw significant recoveries as the markets rebounded later in the year.

The Role of Personality in Investment Choices

Definition An individual's personality traits, such as risk tolerance, confidence, and temperament, play a significant role in their investment decisions. These traits influence how an investor perceives risk, responds to market movements, and makes investment choices.

Impact on Investing
- **Risk Tolerance**: Investors with high risk tolerance are more likely to engage in speculative investments,

seeking higher returns despite the associated risks. Conversely, those with low risk tolerance may prefer conservative strategies to preserve capital.

- **Confidence Levels**: Overly confident investors may take excessive risks, believing they can predict market movements or identify winning investments. Underconfident investors may hesitate to invest, missing out on potential opportunities due to fear of making mistakes.

Examples

- **Aggressive Investors**: A highly confident and risk-tolerant investor might invest heavily in volatile stocks or emerging markets, seeking high returns despite the high risk. This aggressive approach can lead to significant gains, but also substantial losses.
- **Conservative Investors**: An investor with a low risk tolerance and cautious personality may stick to bonds and blue-chip stocks, avoiding potentially higher-return but riskier investments. This conservative approach can provide stability but may result in lower overall returns.

Case Study: Warren Buffett vs. Elon Musk

- **Warren Buffett**: Known for his cautious and calculated investment approach, Buffett's personality reflects a high level of patience and risk aversion. He focuses on long-term value investing and avoids speculative ventures.
- **Elon Musk**: Musk's bold and risk-tolerant personality is evident in his ventures, from Tesla to SpaceX. His confidence and willingness to take significant risks have led to remarkable successes, but also notable failures and volatility.

Managing Emotional Influences

Mindfulness and Emotional Regulation Practicing mindfulness and emotional regulation techniques can help investors manage fear, greed, stress, and anxiety. Techniques such as meditation, deep breathing, and stress management exercises can improve emotional control, leading to better investment decisions.

Setting Clear Investment Goals Having clear, well-defined investment goals provides a framework for making rational decisions and helps avoid impulsive actions driven by emotions. This includes setting long-term financial objectives and sticking to a disciplined investment strategy.

Seeking Professional Advice Consulting with financial advisors can provide an objective perspective and help investors stay disciplined. Advisors can offer guidance that is not influenced by the investor's personal emotions and biases.

Regular Portfolio Reviews Periodic reviews of the investment portfolio ensure that it remains aligned with the investor's goals and risk tolerance. This helps in making necessary adjustments while avoiding emotional reactions to short-term market fluctuations.

Utilizing Automated Investing Tools Automated investing tools and robo-advisors can help mitigate the impact of emotions on investment decisions. These tools use algorithms to manage investments based on predefined criteria, reducing the influence of fear and greed.

Building a Support Network Having a support network of fellow investors or a financial mentor can provide emotional support and guidance during stressful market conditions. Sharing experiences and discussing investment strategies can help in maintaining a rational perspective.

Case Study: Utilizing a Financial Advisor An investor who frequently experiences stress and anxiety about their investment decisions decides to work with a financial advisor. The advisor helps the investor set clear goals, develop a disciplined investment strategy, and provides regular portfolio reviews. This professional guidance helps the investor stay focused on their long-term objectives and avoid impulsive decisions driven by emotions.

Case Study: Automated Investing with Robo-Advisors An investor decides to use a robo-advisor to manage their portfolio. The robo-advisor creates a diversified investment plan based on the investor's risk tolerance and financial goals. By automating the investment process, the investor reduces the impact of their emotions on decision-making and achieves more consistent financial outcomes.

By understanding and managing the emotional influences on investment decisions, investors can enhance their decision-making processes, reduce the impact of irrational behaviors, and achieve more consistent and favorable financial outcomes.

CHAPTER 4

The Psychology of Risk and Uncertainty

Understanding how investors perceive and manage risk is crucial for making informed investment decisions. This chapter delves into the psychological aspects of risk perception, risk tolerance, and strategies for managing risk effectively.

Perception of Risk

Definition Perception of risk refers to how investors view the potential for loss in their investments. This perception is influenced by psychological factors, personal experiences, and individual biases, rather than purely objective assessments. Risk perception can vary significantly among investors, even when faced with the same set of financial circumstances.

Impact on Investing

- **Risk Overestimation**: Some investors may perceive higher risk than actually exists, leading to overly conservative investment choices. This can result in lower returns and missed opportunities for growth.
- **Risk Underestimation**: Others may underestimate risk, leading to excessive risk-taking and potential losses. Underestimating risk can expose investors to significant

financial harm if their investments do not perform as expected.

Examples

- **Market Volatility**: During periods of high market volatility, some investors might overestimate the risk of continued declines, leading them to sell off assets prematurely. This can lock in losses and prevent them from benefiting from a potential market recovery.
- **Stable Markets**: In stable or rising markets, investors might underestimate the risk of a downturn, leading to complacency and a lack of risk management. This can result in substantial losses when the market eventually corrects.

Case Study: The Financial Crisis of 2008 The 2008 financial crisis provides a stark example of how risk perception can impact investment decisions. Prior to the crisis, many investors underestimated the risks associated with subprime mortgages and mortgage-backed securities. The widespread perception that housing prices would continue to rise led to excessive risk-taking. When the housing bubble burst, the underestimated risks became apparent, leading to massive losses and market turmoil.

Risk Tolerance and Risk Capacity

Definition

- **Risk Tolerance**: The degree of variability in investment returns that an investor is willing to withstand. It reflects the investor's comfort level with the ups and downs of the market.
- **Risk Capacity**: The actual ability of an investor to endure financial losses without compromising their financial goals. It considers factors such as income, savings, time horizon, and financial obligations.

Impact on Investing

- **Mismatch Between Tolerance and Capacity**: Investing

in ways that do not align with one's risk tolerance or capacity can lead to financial distress and suboptimal investment outcomes. For example, taking on more risk than one can tolerate or afford can result in panic selling during downturns or inability to meet financial obligations.

Examples

- **Young Investors**: Typically have higher risk tolerance and capacity due to longer time horizons, allowing them to invest more aggressively. They can afford to take on more risk because they have more time to recover from potential losses.
- **Retirees**: Generally have lower risk capacity due to the need for stable income, requiring more conservative investment strategies. Their priority is often capital preservation rather than growth, as they rely on their investments for income.

Case Study: Lifecycle Investing Lifecycle investing strategies adjust risk exposure based on the investor's age and financial situation. Younger investors might hold a higher percentage of stocks, which are riskier but offer higher potential returns. As they approach retirement, the allocation shifts towards bonds and other safer investments, reflecting their decreased risk capacity and need for income stability.

Strategies for Managing Risk

Objective Decision-Making Using structured decision-making frameworks can help manage emotional responses to risk and uncertainty. This includes:

- **Setting Clear Investment Goals**: Clearly defined goals provide a roadmap for investment decisions and help keep investors focused on their long-term objectives.
- **Establishing Risk Management Protocols**: These protocols might include setting stop-loss orders, defining asset allocation limits, and creating a

rebalancing strategy.

- **Adhering to a Disciplined Investment Approach**: Following a disciplined approach, such as sticking to a diversified investment plan, can help investors avoid making impulsive decisions based on short-term market movements.

Diversification Diversification across asset classes, sectors, and geographic regions can mitigate risk by reducing the impact of any single investment's poor performance on the overall portfolio. A well-diversified portfolio spreads risk and can provide more stable returns over time.

Regular Review and Adjustment Periodic review and adjustment of the investment portfolio ensure that it remains aligned with the investor's risk tolerance and financial goals. This process involves:

- **Assessing Current Holdings**: Evaluating the performance of current investments and their alignment with financial goals.
- **Rebalancing**: Adjusting the portfolio to maintain the desired asset allocation and risk level.
- **Considering Market Conditions**: Taking into account changes in market conditions and personal circumstances that might affect the investment strategy.

Use of Hedging Strategies Employing hedging strategies, such as options and futures, can protect against downside risk while allowing participation in market gains. These strategies include:

- **Options**: Contracts that give investors the right, but not the obligation, to buy or sell an asset at a predetermined price within a specified period. Options can be used to hedge against potential losses or to speculate on future price movements.
- **Futures**: Agreements to buy or sell an asset at a future date for a price agreed upon today. Futures can be used

THE PSYCHOLOGY OF INVESTING

to lock in prices and manage risk associated with price fluctuations.

Case Study: Using Hedging to Protect Investments An investor holding a significant position in a tech stock might use options to hedge against potential losses. By purchasing put options, the investor secures the right to sell the stock at a specified price, providing a safety net if the stock price falls. This strategy can help protect against downside risk while maintaining the potential for upside gains.

Behavioral Risk Management Understanding and mitigating the influence of cognitive biases on risk perception is also critical. Techniques include:

- **Awareness and Education**: Learning about common biases, such as overconfidence and loss aversion, can help investors recognize and counteract their effects.
- **Checklists and Decision Rules**: Using checklists and predefined decision rules can reduce the impact of emotions and biases on investment decisions.
- **Seeking Diverse Perspectives**: Consulting with financial advisors or discussing investment strategies with peers can provide additional insights and help challenge biased thinking.

Case Study: Implementing Behavioral Risk Management An investment firm might implement training programs for its advisors on behavioral finance principles. Advisors can use this knowledge to help clients recognize their biases and make more informed decisions. For example, during periods of market volatility, advisors can remind clients of their long-term goals and the importance of staying the course, rather than making impulsive decisions based on short-term fears.

Advanced Strategies for Managing Risk

Dynamic Asset Allocation Dynamic asset allocation involves adjusting the mix of assets in a portfolio based on changing market conditions and economic indicators. This strategy aims to optimize the risk-return profile of the portfolio over time.

Risk Parity Risk parity is an investment strategy that focuses on allocating risk, rather than capital, equally among different assets. This approach seeks to achieve a more balanced and diversified portfolio by ensuring that no single asset class dominates the risk profile.

Tail Risk Hedging Tail risk hedging involves strategies designed to protect against extreme market events, such as market crashes or black swan events. These strategies may include options, futures, or other derivatives that provide protection during severe downturns.

Case Study: Tail Risk Hedging During Market Crashes During the 2008 financial crisis, some investors used tail risk hedging strategies to protect their portfolios. By holding out-of-the-money put options on major indices, they were able to offset losses in their equity holdings when the market plummeted. This approach helped preserve capital during one of the most severe market downturns in history.

By understanding the psychology of risk and uncertainty, investors can better navigate the complexities of the financial markets. Recognizing personal biases, aligning risk tolerance with risk capacity, and employing effective risk management strategies are essential for achieving long-term financial success.

CHAPTER 5

Decision-Making Strategies

Investing involves a series of complex decisions that can significantly impact financial outcomes. This chapter explores the differences between rational and irrational decision-making, techniques to improve decision-making processes, and the role of intuition in investing.

Rational vs. Irrational Decision-Making

Definition Rational decision-making involves logical, methodical, and data-driven choices, relying on careful analysis of available information and consideration of potential outcomes. It is grounded in objective reasoning and systematic evaluation.

Irrational decision-making, on the other hand, is influenced by emotions, cognitive biases, and psychological factors. Decisions made irrationally often lack consistency and may be driven by short-term impulses rather than long-term goals.

Impact on Investing

- **Rational Decisions**: Tend to lead to more consistent and predictable investment outcomes. Rational investors systematically analyze financial data, assess risks, and make decisions based on thorough research and planning.
- **Irrational Decisions**: Can result in erratic investment

behavior, leading to significant financial losses. Irrational investors may react impulsively to market fluctuations, succumb to herd behavior, or make decisions based on unfounded beliefs or emotions.

Examples

- **Rational**: Using fundamental and technical analysis to guide investment choices. For instance, an investor might analyze a company's financial statements, industry position, and market trends before buying its stock.
- **Irrational**: Making investment decisions based on rumors, hype, or panic reactions. An example would be buying a stock solely because it has been heavily promoted on social media, without any underlying analysis of its true value.

Case Study: Rational vs. Irrational Decisions During the COVID-19 Pandemic During the initial stages of the COVID-19 pandemic, markets experienced extreme volatility. Rational investors conducted in-depth analyses of company fundamentals, considering long-term prospects and the impacts of the pandemic. They identified undervalued stocks and made strategic investments. Irrational investors, driven by panic and fear, sold off their assets at significant losses, only to see those same assets rebound strongly as the markets recovered.

Techniques to Improve Decision-Making

Precommitment Strategies Establishing rules and guidelines for investment decisions ahead of time helps prevent emotional reactions during market volatility. Precommitment strategies include:

- **Setting Stop-Loss Orders**: These orders automatically sell a security when its price falls to a certain level, protecting against significant losses.
- **Defining Profit-Taking Levels**: Establishing specific price points at which to sell a security and take profits

can help prevent greed from leading to holding onto a stock for too long.

Seeking Diverse Perspectives Consulting with financial advisors and considering diverse viewpoints can provide a more balanced perspective and counteract personal biases. This involves:

- **Professional Advice**: Financial advisors can offer objective insights and help investors develop strategies that align with their goals and risk tolerance.
- **Peer Discussions**: Engaging in discussions with other investors can introduce different viewpoints and strategies, broadening one's understanding of the market.

Mindfulness and Stress Management Practicing mindfulness and stress management techniques can improve emotional regulation, leading to more rational investment decisions. Techniques include:

- **Meditation and Deep Breathing**: These practices can help reduce stress and anxiety, allowing for clearer thinking and better decision-making.
- **Regular Exercise**: Physical activity can reduce stress hormones and improve overall mental health, contributing to more rational behavior.

Case Study: The Benefits of Precommitment Strategies An investor who sets stop-loss orders and profit-taking levels before entering a trade can avoid making hasty decisions based on emotional reactions to market movements. For example, during a market downturn, their stop-loss order triggers automatically, preventing further losses, while predefined profit-taking levels ensure gains are locked in during a market uptrend.

Case Study: Seeking Professional Advice An investor worried about market volatility decides to consult a financial advisor. The advisor helps the investor set clear financial goals, establish a diversified investment strategy, and provide ongoing support during market fluctuations. By seeking professional advice, the investor gains a more balanced perspective and avoids making impulsive decisions based on short-term market movements.

The Role of Intuition in Investing

Definition Intuition is the ability to understand something instinctively without the need for conscious reasoning. While intuition can be valuable, particularly for experienced investors, it must be balanced with analytical thinking to avoid impulsive decisions.

Impact on Investing

- **Positive**: Experienced investors may develop an intuitive sense of market movements and opportunities based on years of observation and practice. This "gut feeling" can sometimes lead to timely and profitable decisions.
- **Negative**: Overreliance on intuition without supporting analysis can lead to impulsive and poorly informed decisions. For novice investors, intuition can be particularly dangerous if not tempered with thorough research.

Examples

- **Experienced Traders**: May use intuition to identify market trends and entry points based on years of experience. For instance, a trader might sense a market reversal based on subtle indicators that are not immediately obvious from the data.
- **Novice Investors**: Should rely more on structured analysis and advice rather than intuition to avoid common pitfalls. For example, a new investor might feel a strong urge to invest in a hot stock based on media hype, but disciplined analysis could reveal that the stock is overvalued.

Balancing Intuition with Analysis While intuition can be a powerful tool, it should be used in conjunction with analytical methods. Strategies include:

- **Combining Intuition with Data**: Using intuition to generate ideas or hypotheses, which are then validated through rigorous data analysis.
- **Regularly Reviewing Decisions**: Assessing past investment decisions to understand when intuition was accurate and when it led to mistakes, refining the approach over time.

Case Study: Warren Buffett's Approach Warren Buffett is known for his intuitive understanding of businesses and markets, developed over decades of investing. However, his intuition is always supported by meticulous analysis of financial statements, competitive positioning, and management quality. This combination of intuition and analysis has contributed to his long-term success.

Case Study: George Soros and Reflexivity George Soros, a legendary investor, is known for his theory of reflexivity, which emphasizes the impact of market participants' perceptions on market fundamentals. Soros often relies on his intuitive sense of market psychology and trends, but he also supports his decisions with rigorous analysis. This balance of intuition and analysis has led to some of his most successful trades, such as his famous bet against the British pound in 1992.

Conclusion

Effective decision-making in investing requires a balance between rational analysis and intuitive insight. By understanding the differences between rational and irrational decision-making, employing strategies to improve decision-making processes, and appropriately leveraging intuition, investors can enhance their investment outcomes and achieve long-term financial success. Continual education, disciplined approaches, and a willingness to seek diverse perspectives are key components of successful investment strategies.

CHAPTER 6

Overcoming Biases

Cognitive biases can significantly impact investment decisions, often leading to suboptimal outcomes. Understanding and mitigating these biases is crucial for making rational, informed decisions. This chapter explores how to identify personal biases, strategies to mitigate them, and case studies of successful investors who have effectively managed their biases.

Identifying Personal Biases

Definition Identifying personal biases involves recognizing the specific cognitive and emotional biases that influence one's investment decisions. These biases can distort perception and judgment, leading to irrational actions.

Impact on Investing

- **Self-Awareness**: Increases the ability to make more rational and informed investment choices. Recognizing biases allows investors to understand their decision-making patterns and make adjustments.
- **Bias Mitigation**: Helps in developing strategies to counteract the influence of biases. By identifying and acknowledging biases, investors can implement measures to minimize their impact.

Examples

- **Reflection and Journaling**: Keeping a decision journal to track investment decisions and outcomes can help identify recurring biases. By recording the reasoning behind each decision and its subsequent outcome, investors can spot patterns and biases that may be influencing their behavior.
- **Feedback and Analysis**: Regularly reviewing investment performance and seeking feedback from advisors or peers can highlight biases that need addressing. This external perspective can provide valuable insights into how biases are affecting investment choices.

Case Study: Identifying Biases through Journaling An investor keeps a detailed journal of their investment decisions, noting the reasons for each trade, their emotional state, and the outcome. Over time, they notice a pattern of selling stocks prematurely due to fear of loss (loss aversion bias). Recognizing this bias, they implement strategies to hold onto investments longer, resulting in improved returns.

Strategies to Mitigate Biases

Education and Training Continual learning about cognitive biases and their impact on decision-making can help investors recognize and mitigate their effects. This involves:

- **Reading Books and Articles**: Engaging with literature on behavioral finance to understand different types of biases and their effects.
- **Taking Courses and Workshops**: Participating in educational programs focused on decision-making and behavioral finance.

Structured Decision-Making Processes Using systematic approaches to decision-making, such as checklists and algorithms, can reduce the influence of biases. These processes include:

- **Checklists**: Creating detailed checklists for evaluating investment opportunities can ensure that all relevant factors are considered objectively.
- **Algorithms**: Implementing algorithmic trading systems based on predefined rules can help eliminate emotional decision-making.

Accountability Mechanisms Involving accountability partners or advisors in the decision-making process can provide external checks and balances. This includes:

- **Investment Committees**: Forming a committee to review and approve major investment decisions can introduce diverse perspectives and reduce individual biases.
- **Advisory Relationships**: Working with financial advisors who can offer objective advice and help investors stay disciplined.

Case Study: Structured Decision-Making at Bridgewater Associates Ray Dalio, founder of Bridgewater Associates, employs a systematic decision-making process known as "radical transparency." This approach involves rigorous data analysis, checklists, and open discussion of decisions within the firm. By creating a culture where decisions are thoroughly vetted and biases are openly discussed, Bridgewater has managed to achieve consistent investment success.

Tools for Mitigating Biases In addition to educational and structural strategies, various tools can help investors identify and mitigate biases. These include:

- **Behavioral Finance Apps**: Apps like Personal Capital and Mint offer insights into spending and investment behaviors, helping users recognize and adjust for biases.
- **Financial Simulators**: Tools that simulate different market scenarios can help investors understand the potential impact of their biases in various conditions.

- **Psychometric Testing**: Tests designed to reveal individual biases and risk tolerance can provide a clearer understanding of personal investment behavior.

Case Study: Using Financial Simulators An investor uses a financial simulator to test their investment strategies under different market conditions. The simulator reveals that their inclination to hold onto losing stocks (anchoring bias) would have led to significant losses in past bear markets. Armed with this insight, the investor develops a more flexible strategy, including predefined sell rules to avoid such pitfalls in the future.

Case Studies of Successful Investors

Warren Buffett Known for his disciplined investment approach and long-term perspective, Warren Buffett has consistently outperformed the market by avoiding common cognitive biases and focusing on value investing principles. Key strategies include:

- **Sticking to a Core Investment Philosophy**: Buffett adheres to value investing principles, seeking out undervalued companies with strong fundamentals and long-term growth potential.
- **Avoiding Herd Behavior**: Buffett often takes contrarian positions, investing in companies or sectors that are out of favor with the market.
- **Maintaining Patience and Discipline**: Buffett is known for his patience, holding investments for the long term and avoiding the temptation to chase short-term gains.

Case Study: Buffett's Investment in American Express During the 1963 salad oil scandal, American Express's stock price plummeted. While many investors panicked and sold their shares, Buffett saw an opportunity. He recognized that the scandal did not impact the core business model of American Express. By staying disciplined and avoiding the herd mentality, he invested heavily in the company, resulting in significant long-term gains.

Ray Dalio Founder of Bridgewater Associates, Ray Dalio emphasizes radical transparency and systematic decision-making to mitigate biases and improve investment performance. Key strategies include:

- **Radical Transparency**: Encouraging open and honest discussion of investment decisions to identify and mitigate biases.
- **Systematic Processes**: Utilizing data-driven decision-making processes and algorithms to guide investment strategies.
- **Emphasizing Principles**: Dalio's book, "Principles," outlines his approach to decision-making and leadership, focusing on principles that help mitigate biases and promote rational thinking.

Case Study: Ray Dalio's Radical Transparency At Bridgewater Associates, Dalio implemented a culture of radical transparency, where all meetings are recorded, and employees are encouraged to challenge each other's ideas. This open environment helps uncover and address biases, leading to more robust decision-making. For instance, during the 2008 financial crisis, Bridgewater's systematic approach and culture of open dialogue helped the firm navigate the turmoil more effectively than many of its peers.

Advanced Strategies for Mitigating Biases

Behavioral Nudges Implementing behavioral nudges can help steer investors towards better decision-making. Nudges are subtle changes in the way choices are presented, designed to influence behavior without restricting options. Examples include:

- **Default Options**: Automatically enrolling employees in retirement savings plans but allowing them to opt out if they choose. This increases participation rates.
- **Simplified Choices**: Reducing the complexity of investment options to prevent choice overload, which can lead to suboptimal decisions.

Case Study: Behavioral Nudges in Retirement Plans A large corporation implemented a nudge strategy by automatically enrolling new employees in the company's 401(k) plan with a default contribution rate. Employees were free to opt out or change their contribution rate, but the default setting led to higher overall participation and savings rates.

Emotional Regulation Techniques Investors can benefit from techniques designed to manage emotions effectively. These include:

- **Cognitive Behavioral Therapy (CBT)**: A form of psychological treatment that helps individuals recognize and change negative thought patterns. For investors, CBT can be used to manage anxiety and improve decision-making under stress.
- **Mindfulness Meditation**: Regular practice of mindfulness can increase emotional regulation and reduce impulsive decision-making.

Case Study: Using CBT for Investment Decisions An investor struggling with anxiety and impulsive decisions due to market volatility starts practicing CBT. Through this therapy, they learn to identify and challenge their irrational thoughts about market movements, leading to more rational investment decisions and reduced anxiety.

Conclusion

Identifying and mitigating cognitive biases is essential for successful investing. By increasing self-awareness, employing structured decision-making processes, seeking diverse perspectives, and learning from successful investors, individuals can improve their investment decisions and achieve better financial outcomes. Continual education and disciplined strategies are key to overcoming biases and maintaining a rational approach to investing.

Investors who understand their biases and take steps to mitigate them can navigate the complexities of the financial markets more effectively, leading to more consistent and successful investment outcomes.

CHAPTER 7

Practical Applications and Tools

In the digital age, technology offers numerous tools and resources that can help investors make better decisions and reduce the impact of cognitive biases. This chapter explores how leveraging technology, using practical tools, and building a bias-resistant investment strategy can lead to more rational and informed investment decisions.

Using Technology to Reduce Biases

Definition Leveraging technology involves using software and tools to aid in investment decision-making and reduce the influence of biases. These tools can provide objective data, automate processes, and offer insights that help investors make more informed decisions.

Impact on Investing

- **Data-Driven Decisions**: Technology can provide data-driven insights and analytics, improving the accuracy of investment decisions. By relying on factual data rather than emotions or subjective opinions, investors can make more rational choices.
- **Automation**: Automated trading systems can execute trades based on predefined criteria, minimizing emotional interference. This helps ensure that decisions

are consistent and aligned with the investor's strategy, regardless of market volatility.

Examples

- **Robo-Advisors**: Use algorithms to create and manage investment portfolios based on individual risk tolerance and goals. Examples include Betterment, Wealthfront, and Vanguard Personal Advisor Services. These platforms offer personalized investment strategies while minimizing human biases.
- **Analytical Tools**: Platforms like Bloomberg and Morningstar provide comprehensive data and analysis to support informed decision-making. These tools offer financial metrics, historical data, and market analysis that help investors evaluate potential investments objectively.

Case Study: The Rise of Robo-Advisors Robo-advisors have gained popularity for their ability to provide personalized investment advice and portfolio management at a lower cost. By using algorithms and data analytics, robo-advisors minimize the impact of cognitive biases and help investors achieve their financial goals through disciplined and automated strategies. For example, Betterment offers tax-loss harvesting and automatic rebalancing, features that can optimize returns while reducing emotional decision-making.

Tools for Better Decision-Making

Investment Apps Investment apps offer a range of tools for tracking investments, analyzing performance, and executing trades. Popular apps include:

- **Robinhood**: Provides commission-free trading and easy access to financial markets, making it popular among retail investors.
- **E*TRADE**: Offers robust trading tools, educational resources, and a wide range of investment options.
- **Fidelity**: Known for its comprehensive research tools,

investment options, and customer service.

Educational Resources Websites and online platforms provide valuable information and learning opportunities to enhance investment knowledge. Key resources include:

- **Investopedia**: Offers articles, tutorials, and educational content on a wide range of financial topics.
- **Financial News Outlets**: Websites like CNBC, Bloomberg, and Reuters provide up-to-date market news, analysis, and insights.
- **Online Courses**: Platforms like Coursera, Udemy, and Khan Academy offer courses on investing, financial markets, and behavioral finance.

Behavioral Finance Tools Applications that incorporate behavioral finance principles help investors understand their financial behaviors and make better decisions. Examples include:

- **Personal Capital**: Provides financial planning and investment management tools, along with insights into spending patterns and investment performance.
- **Mint**: Helps users track their finances, set budgets, and manage investments, offering a comprehensive view of their financial health.

Case Study: Using Educational Resources to Enhance Decision-Making An investor uses Investopedia to learn about different investment strategies and market dynamics. By regularly reading financial news from Bloomberg and participating in online courses, they gain a deeper understanding of the markets and develop a more informed investment approach. This continuous learning helps them make better decisions and avoid common pitfalls driven by cognitive biases.

Building a Bias-Resistant Investment Strategy

Diversification A well-diversified portfolio spreads risk across various assets, reducing the impact of biases related to overconfidence and risk perception. Diversification involves investing in a mix of asset classes, such as stocks, bonds, real estate, and commodities, to mitigate the risk of significant losses from any single investment.

Regular Portfolio Review Periodic reviews and adjustments ensure the portfolio remains aligned with investment goals and risk tolerance, mitigating the influence of biases over time. This process involves assessing current holdings, rebalancing the portfolio, and considering changes in market conditions and personal circumstances.

Setting Clear Objectives Having clear, well-defined investment objectives provides a framework for making rational decisions and avoiding impulsive actions driven by biases. Objectives should be specific, measurable, achievable, relevant, and time-bound (SMART).

Case Study: The Benefits of Regular Portfolio Reviews An investor conducts quarterly reviews of their portfolio, evaluating performance and rebalancing as needed. During these reviews, they identify any deviations from their investment strategy and make necessary adjustments. This disciplined approach helps them stay focused on their long-term goals and avoid emotional reactions to short-term market fluctuations.

Use of Hedging Strategies Employing hedging strategies, such as options and futures, can protect against downside risk while allowing participation in market gains. These strategies include:

- **Options**: Contracts that give investors the right, but not the obligation, to buy or sell an asset at a predetermined price within a specified period. Options can be used to hedge against potential losses or to speculate on future price movements.
- **Futures**: Agreements to buy or sell an asset at a future date for a price agreed upon today. Futures can be used to lock in prices and manage risk associated with price fluctuations.

Behavioral Risk Management Understanding and mitigating the influence of cognitive biases on risk perception is also critical. Techniques include:

- **Awareness and Education**: Learning about common biases, such as overconfidence and loss aversion, can help investors recognize and counteract their effects.
- **Checklists and Decision Rules**: Using checklists and predefined decision rules can reduce the impact of emotions and biases on investment decisions.
- **Seeking Diverse Perspectives**: Consulting with financial advisors or discussing investment strategies with peers can provide additional insights and help challenge biased thinking.

Case Study: Implementing Behavioral Risk Management An investment firm might implement training programs for its advisors on behavioral finance principles. Advisors can use this knowledge to help clients recognize their biases and make more informed decisions. For example, during periods of market volatility, advisors can remind clients of their long-term goals and the importance of staying the course, rather than making impulsive decisions based on short-term fears.

Advanced Technology and Tools for Investing

Artificial Intelligence (AI) and Machine Learning AI and machine learning can analyze vast amounts of data more quickly and accurately than humans, identifying patterns and trends that may not be immediately apparent. These technologies can:

- **Predict Market Trends**: By analyzing historical data and current market conditions, AI can predict future market movements and suggest optimal investment strategies.
- **Automate Trading**: Machine learning algorithms can execute trades automatically based on predefined criteria, reducing the impact of human biases and emotions.

Blockchain Technology Blockchain technology offers transparency and security, which can help reduce biases related to

trust and information asymmetry. Applications include:
- **Decentralized Finance (DeFi)**: Platforms that use blockchain to provide financial services without intermediaries, increasing transparency and reducing the potential for bias.
- **Smart Contracts**: Automated contracts that execute when certain conditions are met, ensuring that investment decisions are based on predefined criteria rather than emotions.

Virtual Reality (VR) and Augmented Reality (AR) VR and AR can provide immersive experiences that help investors better understand complex financial data and market scenarios. These technologies can:
- **Visualize Data**: Present financial data in a more intuitive and interactive way, making it easier for investors to comprehend and analyze.
- **Simulate Market Conditions**: Allow investors to experience different market conditions and test their strategies in a virtual environment before applying them in the real world.

Case Study: AI-Powered Investment Platforms A financial firm uses an AI-powered platform to manage its investment portfolio. The platform analyzes market data, predicts trends, and executes trades automatically. The firm reports higher returns and lower volatility compared to traditional investment methods, attributing the success to the AI's ability to eliminate emotional biases and make data-driven decisions.

Practical Applications of Behavioral Finance

Behavioral Finance Apps Behavioral finance apps can help investors recognize and mitigate biases by providing insights into their financial behavior. Examples include:
- **Personal Capital**: Tracks spending and investment performance, offering personalized insights and recommendations.

- **PocketSmith**: Helps users project their future financial position based on current spending and investment habits.

Financial Wellness Programs Employers can offer financial wellness programs that educate employees about behavioral finance and help them make better financial decisions. These programs can include:

- **Workshops and Seminars**: Educating employees about common biases and how to avoid them.
- **Personalized Coaching**: Offering one-on-one sessions with financial advisors to help employees develop and stick to their financial plans.

Case Study: Financial Wellness Programs A large corporation implements a financial wellness program for its employees, offering workshops on behavioral finance and personalized coaching sessions. Employees report improved financial decision-making and greater confidence in managing their investments. The program helps reduce common biases such as overconfidence and loss aversion, leading to better financial outcomes for participants.

Building a Comprehensive Investment Strategy

Integrating Technology and Human Insight While technology can provide valuable data and automate processes, human insight remains crucial for interpreting data and making strategic decisions. A comprehensive investment strategy should integrate both:

- **Data-Driven Insights**: Using technology to gather and analyze data, identify trends, and execute trades.
- **Human Judgment**: Leveraging human experience and intuition to interpret data, set strategic goals, and make nuanced decisions.

Continuous Learning and Adaptation The financial markets are dynamic and constantly evolving. Investors must commit to continuous learning and adaptation to stay informed and competitive. This includes:

- **Staying Updated**: Regularly reading financial news, taking courses, and attending seminars to stay current on market developments and investment strategies.
- **Adapting Strategies**: Continuously evaluating and adjusting investment strategies based on new information and changing market conditions.

Case Study: Continuous Learning and Adaptation An investor regularly attends financial seminars and takes online courses to stay updated on the latest market trends and investment strategies. By continuously learning and adapting their approach, the investor remains competitive and achieves consistent long-term success, avoiding common pitfalls and biases that can derail their investment goals.

Conclusion

Recap of Key Points Understanding the psychological aspects of investing, including cognitive biases and emotional influences, is crucial for making rational investment decisions. By recognizing and mitigating these biases, investors can enhance their decision-making processes, improve investment performance, and achieve long-term financial success.

Encouragement for Continuous Learning Investing is a dynamic and ongoing process. Continuous learning and self-awareness are essential for adapting to changing market conditions and personal circumstances. Staying informed about new tools, strategies, and market developments can help investors remain competitive and make better decisions.

Final Thoughts By integrating the principles of behavioral finance into their investment strategies, investors can better navigate the complexities of the financial markets and make smarter, more informed decisions. Leveraging technology, employing structured decision-making processes, and maintaining a disciplined approach are key to overcoming cognitive biases and achieving financial success.

CONCLUSION

Recap Of Key Points

Throughout this book, we have explored the intricate relationship between psychology and investing, highlighting how cognitive biases and emotional influences can significantly impact financial decisions. By understanding these psychological factors and implementing strategies to mitigate their effects, investors can enhance their decision-making processes and achieve better financial outcomes.

1. **The Psychology of Investing**: Recognizing the importance of psychological factors in investment decisions and how biases can distort rational thinking.
2. **Common Cognitive Biases**: Identifying and understanding common biases such as overconfidence, confirmation bias, anchoring, loss aversion, and herd behavior, and their impact on investing.
3. **Emotional Influences**: Exploring how emotions like fear, greed, stress, and anxiety affect investment choices and strategies to manage these emotions.
4. **Risk and Uncertainty**: Understanding risk perception, risk tolerance, and effective risk management strategies, including diversification and hedging.
5. **Decision-Making Strategies**: Differentiating between rational and irrational decision-making, leveraging intuition appropriately, and using precommitment

strategies to improve investment decisions.
6. **Overcoming Biases**: Techniques for identifying personal biases, structured decision-making processes, accountability mechanisms, and learning from successful investors.
7. **Practical Applications and Tools**: Utilizing technology, investment apps, educational resources, and behavioral finance tools to build a bias-resistant investment strategy.

Learning And Improvement

Investing is not a static endeavor; it is a dynamic and ever-evolving field that requires continuous learning and adaptation. The financial markets are influenced by countless factors, including economic trends, geopolitical events, technological advancements, and shifts in investor sentiment. To stay competitive and make informed decisions, investors must commit to lifelong learning and self-improvement.

1. **Stay Informed**: Regularly consume financial news, market analysis, and research reports. Subscribe to reputable financial news outlets and follow thought leaders in the investment community.
2. **Educational Resources**: Take advantage of online courses, webinars, and workshops on investing, behavioral finance, and market analysis. Platforms like Coursera, Udemy, and Khan Academy offer valuable learning opportunities.
3. **Professional Development**: Consider obtaining certifications such as the Chartered Financial Analyst (CFA) designation or other relevant credentials to deepen your investment knowledge and skills.
4. **Networking and Mentorship**: Engage with other investors, join investment clubs, and seek mentorship

from experienced professionals. Learning from others' experiences can provide new perspectives and insights.
5. **Reflect and Adapt**: Regularly review your investment decisions and outcomes. Reflect on what worked well and what didn't, and adapt your strategies accordingly. Keeping a decision journal can help track your progress and identify areas for improvement.
6. **Mindfulness and Emotional Regulation**: Practice mindfulness and stress management techniques to maintain emotional control during volatile market conditions. Techniques such as meditation, deep breathing, and regular exercise can enhance your mental resilience.
7. **Leverage Technology**: Utilize investment apps, robo-advisors, and analytical tools to enhance your decision-making processes. Stay updated on the latest technological advancements that can aid in investment management.

Final Thoughts

The journey to becoming a successful investor is a continuous process of learning, self-discovery, and adaptation. By understanding the psychological aspects of investing and implementing strategies to mitigate biases, you can make more rational and informed decisions. Leveraging technology, maintaining a disciplined approach, and committing to ongoing education are key to navigating the complexities of the financial markets.

Remember, investing is not just about achieving financial gains; it is about making thoughtful, informed decisions that align with your long-term goals and values. Embrace the principles of behavioral finance, stay curious, and keep striving for improvement. With dedication and persistence, you can overcome biases, manage risks effectively, and achieve long-term financial success.

GLOSSARY

Anchoring Bias: The tendency to rely heavily on the first piece of information encountered (the "anchor") when making decisions. In investing, this often manifests as an undue emphasis on the initial purchase price of an investment.

Behavioral Finance: A subfield of finance that explores how psychological influences and cognitive biases affect the financial behaviors of investors and financial practitioners.

Cognitive Biases: Systematic patterns of deviation from rationality that affect judgments and decisions. In investing, these biases can lead to suboptimal financial outcomes.

Confirmation Bias: The tendency to search for, interpret, and remember information in a way that confirms one's preexisting beliefs or hypotheses, leading to selective gathering of evidence.

Diversification: An investment strategy that involves spreading risk across various assets, sectors, and geographic regions to reduce the impact of any single investment's poor performance on the overall portfolio.

Emotional Regulation: Techniques such as meditation, deep breathing, and stress management exercises that help manage emotions like fear and greed, leading to better investment decisions.

Hedging: Using financial instruments such as options and futures to protect against potential losses or to speculate on future price movements.

Herd Behavior: The tendency to follow and mimic the actions of a larger group, whether rational or irrational, which can lead to bubble formations or panic selling in investing.

Intuition: The ability to understand something instinctively without the need for conscious reasoning. While valuable, it must be balanced with analytical thinking in investing.

Loss Aversion: The tendency for people to prefer avoiding losses rather than acquiring equivalent gains, suggesting that the pain of losing is psychologically twice as powerful as the pleasure of gaining.

Overconfidence Bias: The tendency for people to overestimate their knowledge, abilities, and the accuracy of their information, often leading to excessive trading and risk-taking in investing.

Risk Capacity: The actual ability of an investor to endure financial losses without compromising their financial goals, considering factors such as income, savings, time horizon, and financial obligations.

Risk Tolerance: The degree of variability in investment returns that an investor is willing to withstand, reflecting their comfort level with the ups and downs of the market.

Robo-Advisors: Automated platforms that use algorithms to create and manage investment portfolios based on individual risk tolerance and goals, minimizing human biases.

Structured Decision-Making: Systematic approaches to decision-making, such as checklists and algorithms, that reduce the influence of biases and emotions.

Volatility: The degree of variation of a trading price series over time, often measured by standard deviation. High volatility typically indicates high risk.

REFERENCES

Books
- Kahneman, D. (2011). Thinking, Fast and Slow. New York: Farrar, Straus and Giroux.
- Thaler, R. H., & Sunstein, C. R. (2008). Nudge: Improving Decisions About Health, Wealth, and Happiness. New Haven: Yale University Press.
- Dalio, R. (2017). Principles: Life and Work. New York: Simon & Schuster.
- Malkiel, B. G. (2015). A Random Walk Down Wall Street: The Time-Tested Strategy for Successful Investing. New York: W.W. Norton & Company.

Articles and Journals
- Barberis, N., & Thaler, R. (2003). A Survey of Behavioral Finance. Handbook of the Economics of Finance, 1, 1053-1128.
- Shiller, R. J. (2000). Irrational Exuberance. Princeton: Princeton University Press.
- Shefrin, H. (2000). Beyond Greed and Fear: Understanding Behavioral Finance and the Psychology of Investing. Boston: Harvard Business School Press.

Websites and Online Resources
- Investopedia: www.investopedia.com
- Coursera: www.coursera.org
- Khan Academy: www.khanacademy.org
- Udemy: www.udemy.com
- Personal Capital: www.personalcapital.com

- Mint: www.mint.com
- Bloomberg: www.bloomberg.com
- Reuters: www.reuters.com
- CNBC: www.cnbc.com

Software and Tools

- Betterment: www.betterment.com
- Wealthfront: www.wealthfront.com
- Vanguard Personal Advisor Services: personal.vanguard.com
- Robinhood: www.robinhood.com
- E*TRADE: www.etrade.com
- Fidelity: www.fidelity.com

These resources offer a foundation for further study and application of the principles discussed in this book. By continually expanding your knowledge and leveraging the available tools, you can navigate the complexities of investing more effectively.

www.ingramcontent.com/pod-product-compliance
Lightning Source LLC
Chambersburg PA
CBHW071844210526
45479CB00001B/278